CUBA
the people

April Fast and Susan Hughes
Consulting Author Dr. Keith Ellis

Principal photography by Marc Crabtree

A Bobbie Kalman Book
The Lands, Peoples, and Cultures Series

Crabtree Publishing Company
www.crabtreebooks.com

The Lands, Peoples, and Cultures Series

Created by Bobbie Kalman

Coordinating editor
Ellen Rodger

Project editor
Carrie Gleason

Production coordinator
Rosie Gowsell

Project development, design, editing, and photo research
First Folio Resource Group, Inc.
  Erinn Banting
  Quinn Banting
  Molly Bennett
  Tom Dart
  Claire Milne
  Jaimie Nathan
  Debbie Smith
  Meighan Sutherland
  Anikó Szocs

Prepress and printing
Worzalla Publishing Company

Consulting Author
Dr. Keith Ellis, Professor Emeritus, University of Toronto,
Doctor Honoris Causa, University of Havana

Consultants
Grenville Draper, Florida International University, Department
of Geology; John Kirk, Department of Spanish, Dalhousie
University

Photographs
AFP/Corbis/magmaphoto.com: p. 13 (top); Bettmann/
Corbis/magmaphoto.com: p. 11 (right); Marc Crabtree: title
page, p. 4 (all), p. 6 (left), p. 9 (right), p. 10 (left), p. 12 (left), p.
13 (bottom), p. 14, p. 15 (both), p. 16 (bottom), p. 17 (both), p.
18 (both), p. 19 (both), p. 20, p. 21 (both), p. 22 (left), p. 23 (top),
p. 24 (both), p. 25 (top), p. 26 (left), p. 27 (both), p. 28 (both), p.
29 (both), p. 30, p. 31 (both); Bill Gentile/
Corbis/magmaphoto.com: p. 22 (right); Gavin Hellier/
ImageState: cover; Hulton Archive/Getty Images: p. 7, p. 12

(right); Museo Naval, Madrid, Spain/Bridgeman Art Library:
p.9 (left); Mike King/Corbis/magmaphoto.com: p. 26 (right);
Amos Nachoum/Corbis/magmaphoto.com: p. 3; New York
Historical Society, New York, U.S.A./Bridgeman Art Library:
p. 10 (right); North Wind Picture Archives: p. 6 (right), p. 8;
Reuters NewMedia Inc./Corbis/magmaphoto.com: p.11 (left);
Pascal Rossigno/Reuters NewMedia
Inc./Corbis/magmaphoto.com: p. 25 (bottom); Ulrike Welsch:
p. 16 (top), p. 23 (bottom)

Illustrations
Dianne Eastman: icon
David Wysotski, Allure Illustrations: back cover

Cover: A Cuban woman wears a colorful costume to a parade.
The ruffled sleeves on Cuban costumes flutter as people dance.

Title page: Students relax after school in Havana, Cuba's
capital city.

Icon: *Bohíos*, which are homes made from the leaves and
trunks of royal palm trees, appear at the head of each section.
Royal palm trees grow to be 80 feet (24 meters) tall, and often
only one is needed to build an entire *bohío*.

Back cover: *Almiquí*, or Cuban solenodons, hide during the
day in hollow trees or underground burrows and come out
at night to search for insects and spiders to eat.

Published by
Crabtree Publishing Company

PMB 16A,	612 Welland Avenue	73 Lime Walk
350 Fifth Avenue	St. Catharines	Headington
Suite 3308	Ontario, Canada	Oxford OX3 7AD
New York	L2M 5V6	United Kingdom
N.Y. 10118		

Cataloging-in-Publication data

Hughes, Susan, 1960-
  Cuba. The people / Susan Hughes & April Fast.
    p. cm. -- (Lands, peoples & cultures)
  Includes index.
    ISBN 0-7787-9325-7 (RLB) -- ISBN 0-7787-9693-0 (pbk)
    1. Cuba--History--Juvenile literature. 2. Cuba--Social
life and customs--Juvenile literature. I. Fast, April, 1968-
II. Title. III. Lands, peoples, and cultures series.
    F1776.H86 2004
    972.91--dc22
                                        2004000809
                                           LC

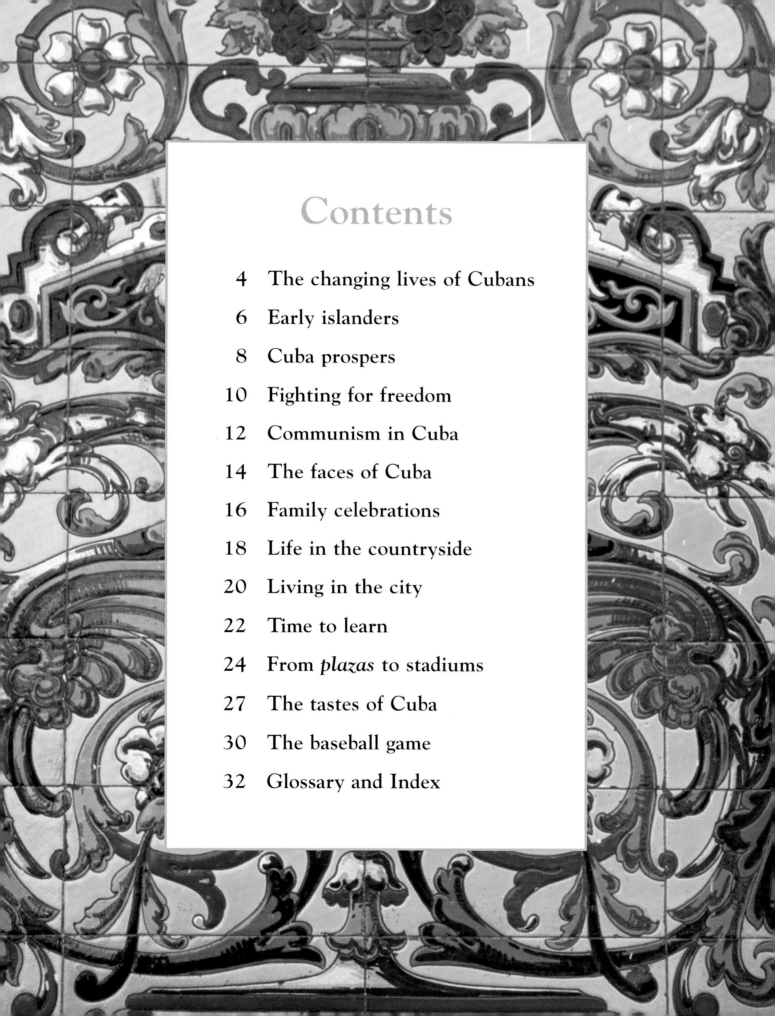

Contents

The changing lives of Cubans

Cuba is an archipelago, or group of islands, in the Caribbean Sea. The people of Cuba sometimes call themselves an *ajiaco*, which is a traditional Cuban stew. Like the stew, which is made up of many different ingredients, Cubans are **descended** from a mixture of peoples, including Europeans, Africans, and Asians.

People buy books and magazines at a stall in Santa Clara, a city in central Cuba. Education is free for all Cubans, so almost everyone can read.

Times of struggle

Cubans have faced many challenges throughout their history. During Spain's 400-year rule of Cuba, both Britain and the United States fought for control of the island. Even after Cuba achieved independence in 1902, the country faced problems as political leaders fought one another to control the government. Some leaders were **dictators**, including Fulgencio Batista, who forcefully took control of Cuba in 1933 and ruled with complete power. Cubans were unhappy with Batista because he did not improve their **standard of living** despite his promises to give them a better life.

Revolution

In 1959, a young lawyer named Fidel Castro and a group of **revolutionaries** overthrew Batista's government. In April 1961, the Cuban government, under Castro, declared Cuba a **Communist** country. In a Communist country, the government owns and controls all the farms, businesses, and industries, and provides the people with housing, health care, and education programs.

Cuba's changing government

Since Castro came to power, Cuba has faced many hardships. One of the greatest obstacles has been the economic **embargo** launched by the United States when the Cuban government took over American-owned businesses in Cuba. According to the rules of the embargo, Americans, their **allies**, and any other country that wanted American support or aid was forbidden to trade with Cuba. These restrictions led to severe shortages of food and goods in Cuba.

Today, both the Cuban and United States governments have relaxed some of the rules. Certain industries in the United States are allowed to trade with Cuba, and the U.S. cannot stop other countries, such as China and Canada, from trading with Cuba. Castro's government also allows foreign companies to **invest** in Cuban businesses and to own 49 percent of them.

(left) Cousins take a stroll in Parque Central, or Central Park, in Havana, Cuba's capital city.

(top) A couple in Camagüey, in central Cuba, prepares a delicious meal for their family.

5

Archaeologists believe the Ciboney and the Guanahatabey were the first peoples to arrive in Cuba more than 5,000 years ago. They made their homes in caves along the western coast and on some of the southern *cayos*, or islands. They survived by gathering wild fruit and trapping fish, turtles, and iguanas. Shells, bones, and stone tools have been found in caves where the Ciboney lived.

The Taíno, part of a larger group of people called the Arawak, arrived from South America around 1200 B.C. The Taíno caught crabs and fish along Cuba's coasts and hunted for iguanas, birds, and *hutía*, small mammals native to Cuba. They also grew fruit and vegetables, such as yams, corn, beans, and a root vegetable called *yuca*, or cassava.

Caves decorated with images of people, animals, and weapons give clues about the lives of early Cuban settlers.

In this illustration, Christopher Columbus is greeted by Taíno villagers.

The arrival of the Spanish

On October 27, 1492, explorer Christopher Columbus landed on Cuba's shores. He claimed the island for the Spanish king and queen, who had paid for his voyage. When Christopher Columbus met the Taíno, he noticed that some of them wore necklaces with large gold nuggets. When he asked where they had found the gold, they pointed toward the mountains in the center of the island and said *"cubanacán,"* which means "center place." Cuba's name comes from a shortened version of this Taíno word.

Spanish rule

In 1511, Spanish **conquistador** Diego Velázquez de Cuéllar was made governor, or ruler, of Cuba. By 1512, he had established the first Spanish settlement, Baracoa, on the eastern coast. As more Spanish **colonists** arrived, Velázquez built new settlements. The Spanish enslaved the Taíno and forced them to work in gold mines. The Taíno slaves were treated harshly, and thousands died from overwork, starvation, and diseases brought by the Spanish.

Hatuey

The Spanish established colonies on other Caribbean islands before they settled in Cuba. Some Taíno from those islands fled to Cuba so that they would not be enslaved by the Spanish. Hatuey was a *cacique*, or Taíno leader, from the nearby island of Hispaniola. He and 400 of his people escaped to Cuba, and warned the Taíno there about the Spanish.

When Diego Velázquez arrived with Spanish settlers to build Baracoa, Hatuey led the Taíno fight against them. The Taíno's bows and arrows were no match for the guns that the Spanish used, and the Spanish won the battle. Those Taíno who were not killed in battle, including Hatuey, were captured and executed, or put to death. Today, Hatuey is considered a national hero because he fought for the freedom of his people.

Slavery

The Spanish did not find much gold in Cuba, but they discovered that the soil was good for growing crops such as sugar cane and tobacco. Taíno slaves were moved from mines to large farms called **plantations**.

As the Taíno population began to die out and plantations grew, the Spanish brought hundreds of thousands of African slaves to the island because they needed more laborers. Working and living conditions for the slaves were horrible. They were forced to work as many as nineteen hours a day, and were whipped if it was thought that they did not work hard enough. Some Taíno and West African slaves escaped to the countryside or other islands in the Caribbean. Those who did not escape were forced to live in *barracones*, buildings with mud floors and holes in the walls for windows. As many as 200 slaves lived in each *barracon*.

In this illustration, slaves are put into the hold, or lower level, of a ship before being transported to Cuba.

 # Cuba prospers

In the 1500s, Cuba became a busy stop-over for ships traveling from the Caribbean to Europe. Cuba's cities developed along the coasts where natural harbors provided a safe place for ships to dock.

Havana
The northwestern city of Havana, founded in 1519, became the most important port in Cuba. Spanish ships carrying gold and riches from South America and Mexico stopped in Havana to get supplies and to join a flotilla before

heading home to Spain. Flotillas were groups of ships that sailed together for protection against pirates, who were trying to steal the ship's treasures. Sailors were sometimes forced to wait for months until there were enough ships for a flotilla. Hotels, restaurants, markets, and shops were all established in Havana for the waiting sailors.

(top) Ships carrying goods from South and Central America approach Havana's harbor, in this illustration from the 1500s.

Pirates

Between the 1500s and early 1800s, pirates and privateers sailed the Caribbean Sea looking for ships to attack. Pirates made a large **profit** by selling the gold, silver, jewels, and slaves that they stole to European **merchants**. Privateers were given the right to attack the ships of their enemies and take their cargoes by the kings of countries such as England and Spain. Among the most famous pirates and privateers in the Caribbean were Jacques de Sores and Henry Morgan.

Pirates and privateers also attacked cities. In the 1500s, Jacques de Sores attacked Santiago de Cuba, in the southeast, and Havana several times. To protect their goods and people, both cities built forts. Havana's fort, El Morro, was constructed in 1589 at the entrance to the harbor. After pirates and **invaders** attacked in the 1600s and 1700s, another fort called La Punta was built opposite El Morro. Chains and logs were extended from one fort to the other to stop invading ships from entering the harbor.

Construction of El Morro took more than 40 years. In 1845, a lighthouse was built to warn approaching ships of the rocky shore. Today, El Morro is a national monument that is open to the public.

Trade and rebellion

Spain controlled all of Cuba's trade in the 1600s, forcing Cuban plantation owners to sell their crops only to Spain. Spain sold the crops to other countries for a much higher price and made a lot of money. Cuban plantation owners demanded the right to sell their goods directly to other countries, but Spain refused. By the early 1700s, **rebellions** against Spain broke out across the island.

British involvement

Britain saw how wealthy Spain had become from Cuba's crops and wanted part of the profits. It also wanted access to Cuba's ports, especially Havana, so it could increase its own trade. In 1761, Britain declared war on Spain and, by 1762, controlled Havana. The British allowed Cubans to trade with other countries in Europe and with British colonies in North America. Plantation owners made more money and brought thousands more slaves from West Africa to work in Cuba's fields.

In 1763, Britain returned Cuba to Spain in exchange for land in the United States. To prevent a rebellion, Spain allowed Cuban plantation owners to continue trading with British colonies.

In this illustration from 1762, a Spanish ship is sunk as the British invade Havana's harbor.

In the 1800s, many Cubans began to speak out against slavery, demanding that it be abolished, or ended. Cubans also wanted independence from Spain. On October 10, 1868, a rebellion broke out in eastern Cuba when Carlos Manuel de Céspedes and 37 other landowners freed their slaves and declared Cuba's independence. The rebellion turned into a conflict known as the Ten Years' War, which ended with a **cease-fire** in 1878.

José Martí, who led the 1895 rebellion against Spain, was killed in battle. Today, Martí is considered a national hero and is remembered with many statues and streets named in his honor.

Revolution and the United States

Spain agreed to some changes after the Ten Years' War, such as a promise to end slavery, but it refused to grant Cuba independence. In 1895, the Cuban Revolutionary Party, a **nationalist** group founded by Cuban writer José Martí, declared itself leader of an independent Cuba. This declaration started another war with Spain that lasted three years.

The U.S.S. *Maine*

In 1898, the United States sent a battleship to Havana to protect American citizens who had bought Cuban land during the 1800s. The battleship, called the U.S.S. *Maine*, blew up in the harbor. The Americans blamed the Spanish and declared war on Spain. The conflict, which lasted three months, came to be known as the Spanish-American War. When the war was over, the United States took control of Cuba.

An explosion destroys the U.S.S. Maine in Havana's harbor, in this illustration from 1898.

In 1903, the United States leased an area of land on Guantánamo Bay, in southeastern Cuba, for a naval base. The base is still in operation even though the Cuban government wants the United States to return the land.

The road to freedom

The American military stayed in Cuba for four years after the Spanish-American War. The U.S. helped keep the peace, and in 1902 helped Cuba create a new **constitution**. Cubans were allowed to govern themselves, but the United States remained involved in Cuba's affairs with other countries. The U.S. also had the right to buy or **lease** land in Cuba for **naval bases**.

Struggle for power

Even with a new constitution that allowed Cubans to vote for a leader, control of the government changed hands many times because people disagreed with the way the country was being run.

Then, in the 1920s, demand for sugar dropped, and Cuban plantation owners could not make enough money to support their businesses and families. Americans bought many of the plantations and, by the 1930s, American companies owned two-thirds of Cuba's farms, sugar mills, and factories.

President Fulgencio Batista

In 1933, a general named Fulgencio Batista took control of the government with the help of the Cuban army. For seven years, Batista appointed presidents, but he made decisions about how to run the country. In 1940, Batista was elected president. During his rule, he did little to improve life for the Cuban people. He refused to spend money on education, food, and housing, and he allowed foreign companies to operate in Cuba, even though they did not pay Cuban workers fairly. Thousands of people who criticized Batista's government were killed or kidnapped by the army.

In this photograph from the 1950s, Fulgencio Batista speaks to crowds of Cubans gathered outside his palace.

Communism in Cuba

In 1952, Fulgencio Batista cancelled the elections and began to rule as a dictator, without the support of the Cuban people. A group of Cuban revolutionaries began a series of attacks against Batista, including one led by Fidel Castro on July 26, 1953. The attack failed and Castro was put in jail, but many Cubans began to support Castro and the revolution.

Fidel Castro

When Fidel Castro was released from jail in 1955, he went to Mexico to plan further attacks against Batista. In 1956, he returned to Cuba, camped in the Sierra Maestra mountains, in the southeast, and started a war against Batista's government with a group of revolutionaries. Many soldiers on both sides were killed, but as the fighting continued, more people joined Castro's forces.

Cheering Cubans crowd the streets of Havana following the announcement of Batista's removal from power, in this photograph from 1959.

The Cuban Revolution

On January 1, 1959, Fidel Castro and the revolutionaries gained control of Havana. Fulgencio Batista fled the country, and Castro established a new government. He made education and health care free for all Cubans, and nationalized Cuba's plantations, which meant that all farmland, including that owned by Americans, became the property of the Cuban government. The owners were not paid for the loss of their property.

Trade embargo

The United States was upset with Cuba for taking control of American citizens' land on the island. The U.S. government decided to restrict, or do less, business with Cuba. Cuba nationalized all businesses and turned to the Union of Soviet Socialist Republics (U.S.S.R.), an enemy of the United States, for trade. In 1960, the American government declared a trade embargo on Cuba. This meant that no goods could be traded between the United States and Cuba.

These wax statues of Camilo Cienfuegos (left) and Che Guevara (right) stand in a museum in Havana. Che Guevara was a doctor from Argentina who supported many revolutions throughout Latin America. He helped set up the Cuban government once Castro took control and is considered a revolutionary hero today.

The Cuban Missile Crisis

Tensions grew between the United States and the U.S.S.R. The Americans suspected that the U.S.S.R. was going to launch **nuclear missiles** at the U. S. from sites in Cuba. In October 1962, the American government warned the U.S.S.R. that if it did not remove the missiles from Cuba, it would bomb the U.S.S.R. The U.S.S.R. agreed to take down the launch sites and return all the missiles to its country. This was called "the October Crisis" in Cuba or "the Cuban Missile Crisis" by the United States.

The Special Period

The U.S.S.R. collapsed in 1991, leaving Cuba without its main trading partner. Since then, the Cuban people have faced shortages of food, medicine, and fuel. Castro has called this time "the Special Period in a Time of Peace." During this "Special Period," Castro has asked Cubans to find new ways to overcome shortages and to be patient through their country's difficulties. The Cuban government now allows some people to own family-run businesses, and it lets foreign companies invest in Cuban businesses. Increased tourism has also helped Cuba's **economy**.

In April 1961, the United States hired Cuban soldiers who had left the island after Castro came to power to overthrow Castro's government. These soldiers invaded Cuba in a battle known as "the Bay of Pigs" invasion, but they were defeated.

In the 1990s, more tourists from Europe and Canada began to visit Cuba. The government now allows Cubans to set up a small number of independent businesses for tourists, including hotels, restaurants, and resorts.

 # The faces of Cuba

More than eleven million people live in Cuba. Most are descended from the Spanish, African, or Taíno, and a small number have **ancestors** from China. Other people have moved to Cuba from the nearby Caribbean islands of Jamaica, Puerto Rico, and Hispaniola.

The Spanish

Spanish, which is the country's official language, was brought to the island by the Spanish, as was **Roman Catholicism**, a religion practiced by 23 percent of the population. Cuban forms of music, such as *salsa*, use Spanish guitars and melodies. Dishes such as *arroz con pollo*, or chicken with rice, are as popular in Cuba as they are in Spain.

The West Africans

West Africans, who were brought to Cuba as slaves, had a large impact on Cuba's culture. Drums invented in Cuba, such as the bongo and conga drums, are similar to those played in West Africa. They are used in countless styles of Cuban music and dance to keep the strong, lively beat.

(top) A group of young Cubans rest on a bench in Santa Clara, in central Cuba.

Drumming is also important in Santería ceremonies. Santería, which combines West African beliefs with Roman Catholicism, is the most widely practiced religion in Cuba. It developed because Spanish plantation owners forced slaves to give up their religious beliefs and become Roman Catholic. The slaves continued to follow their religions in secret. They renamed their *orishas*, or goddesses and gods, after Christian **saints** so that when plantation owners saw them praying, they thought the slaves were practicing Roman Catholicism.

The French

French colonists moved to Cuba in two waves in the late 1700s and early 1800s. The first wave arrived from Haiti, a country on the island of Hispaniola, during the Haitian people's fight for independence from France. The second wave arrived in 1812 after the Louisiana Purchase, when France sold Louisiana to the United States. The French influence in Cuba can still be felt in communities where people speak Haitian Creole, a language that combines French, English, and Spanish.

Those who leave

When Fidel Castro took over Cuba, more than 250,000 Cubans fled the island, mainly to the United States. Some had supported or worked for Batista's government. Others feared for their futures. When Castro introduced Communism, even more Cubans left, and Castro began to restrict **emigration** from the island. In 1965 and 1980, Castro allowed two large waves of emigrants to leave Cuba because they were unhappy with their government, but they had to leave their possessions behind. The majority of the emigrants went to live with relatives in the United States.

Most other Cubans left the island illegally by sailing on homemade rafts to Florida. Others were **smuggled** into the United States by people already living there. An agreement between the United States and Cuba allows 20,000 Cubans to move to the U.S. every year, but few of the emigrants are given **visas**.

Many Santería ceremonies use West African styles of drums and drumming. The strong drum beats are also part of many types of Cuban music.

Cuban-Americans

There are about 1.5 million Cubans in the United States, and most live in southern Florida. With such a large community, they are able to keep their culture alive. They celebrate traditional Cuban festivals and continue to speak Spanish. Some have become American citizens and plan to remain in the United States. Others look forward to returning to Cuba when a new government takes over.

Cubans in the United States work hard to make the American government aware of what life is like for Cubans in Cuba so they can influence American policy. They run for political office and form organizations to help Cubans new to the U.S. find homes, education, and jobs.

A boy who lives with his parents in Florida visits his grandmother in Cuba.

Children play tug-of-war at a rumbone, *or street party, in Havana.*

In the past, brides and grooms rented their wedding outfits, but today, many save up to buy them or have a family member make them.

In many Cuban neighborhoods, aunts, uncles, cousins, and grandparents live together in one home because affordable housing is difficult to find, despite programs funded by the government. The neighborhoods, or *barrios*, are lively places, especially when families get together to celebrate special occasions at *rumbones*, or street parties. They hang strings of colorful lights from trees, set up rows of tables and chairs, and eat a meal that everyone helps prepare. After the meal, people sing to the music of drums, guitars, and *maracas*, which are **gourds** that rattle with seeds or pebbles.

Palacios de los matrimonios

Some Cuban weddings take place at churches, but most Cubans marry at *palacios de los matrimonios*, or "wedding palaces." Every city in Cuba has at least one of these large, fancy buildings, which used to be the homes of wealthy Cubans. The revolutionary government opened the first *palacios* so that weddings would be affordable for everyone. After the ceremony, families celebrate with parties at the couples' homes or at halls.

Quince

When Cuban girls turn fifteen, they have a special party called a *quince*, which means "fifteen." Fifteen is the age at which girls are considered old enough to begin dating. In cities, *quinces* often take place in special halls called *casas de quince*, or "fifteen houses." In the countryside, people celebrate in their homes, at churches, or in hotels. The birthday girls dress up in gowns that are often as fancy as wedding dresses, and get their hair specially styled for photographs. After the photographs are taken, families host large parties at which they serve birthday cakes decorated with ribbons.

A family celebrates Mother's Day, which is the second Sunday in May. On Mother's Day, the Correos de Cuba, or Cuban Postal Service, prints 1.5 million cards that children mail to their mothers. On the same day, Cubans mark the day in 1955 when Fidel Castro was released from jail.

Families often save up for an entire year to rent or buy quince *dresses that are decorated with lace, ribbons, and pearls.*

Family names

In Cuba, as in most Central and South American countries, people follow the Spanish tradition of giving their children three names — a first name, their father's last name, and their mother's last name. For example, a child named Julio whose father's last name is García and whose mother's last name is Valdés would be named Julio García Valdés.

Life in the countryside

Villages and towns are nestled throughout Cuba's mountains, valleys, rainforests, and plains. Most villages are small, with homes, a school, a small hospital or medical clinic, a cultural center where music and theater performances take place, a few shops, and some grocery stores.

Grocery stores are not the only places to buy food and drinks. Some villagers serve snacks and drinks right out of windows in their homes. People walking, cycling, or traveling on carts pulled by donkeys stop by for a treat.

Rural homes

Village homes are usually made of wood with clay tiled roofs. Many homes have patios and balconies so people can sit outside and enjoy the warm weather. Further out in the countryside are *bohíos* like the ones in which the Taíno lived. Sometimes, several *bohíos* are built close together to form a small community.

(above) Many homes in the mountains have tightly woven roofs made in the same style as the roofs of bohíos. The roofs help keep rain and wind from getting into the homes.

(below) When the Cuban government took control of plantations, many fell into disrepair. Some were divided into smaller plots of land and given to individual farmers.

Plantations

Many plantations built by the Spanish still stand in Cuba's countryside. At one time, the plantations had vast fields, *barracones*, or slaves' quarters, mills or processing plants, and large homes where landowners lived with their families. The homes were sometimes built on posts so that animals and supplies could be sheltered underneath. Wealthy landowners decorated their homes with expensive furniture, and they hired artists to paint colorful frescoes, or images on wet, plastered walls.

State-run farms

After slavery ended, *campesinos*, or peasants, worked on the plantations and harvested different crops in different seasons. For example, they worked on coffee plantations for one part of the year and sugar cane plantations for another part of the year.

Today, many *campesinos* either own small plots of land or they work on state-run farms. *Campesinos* now earn good salaries, and they are paid to go to school if they choose.

(above) Some farms and plantations are used to raise livestock, or farm animals, for their meat, hides, and milk. Vaqueros, or cowboys, herd the animals on horseback.

Horse-drawn buggies are used in many parts of the countryside to travel from place to place.

Living in the city

In Cuban cities, music drifts out of the open windows of homes and stores. Chess and domino players compete in shady parks as people hurry past on their way to work or school. Vendors all over sell snacks, such as corn fritters, to passersby.

Life in a *plaza*
Spanish colonists built many of Cuba's cities to look like cities in Spain. Homes, schools, churches, and businesses surrounded large open *plazas*, or squares. As cities grew, more *plazas* were built so people had a central location where they could relax and meet with friends. Today's *plazas*, which are often filled with beautiful fountains and gardens, are also used to hold large festivals and celebrations. One favorite treat for Cubans who visit *plazas* is ice cream from *Coppelia*, a chain of ice cream restaurants.

(top) Surrounding many plazas are movie theaters, art galleries, and casas de trova, or clubs where bands play a type of music called trova.

Old and new
Most Cuban cities have old sections, where there are buildings from the original Spanish settlements. Mansions that once belonged to wealthy families in old parts of cities are now divided into apartments where many families live. People in cities also live in small homes. Since the revolution, the Cuban government has tried to find ways to build affordable housing for its people, including constructing homes in the suburbs that are made from prefabricated sections, or sections that are built in a factory and assembled at the building site.

Getting around
There are few cars on Cuba's streets. Cuba does not have the materials and factories to build new cars, nor the money to **import** cars from places such as Japan or Germany. In addition, because of the trade embargo, Cubans cannot buy new cars from the United States and fuel is very expensive. Cars in Cuba are 40 or 50 years old. Instead of driving, people usually travel by bicycle, bus, or foot. There are also three-wheeled bicycle taxis. The driver sits on a bicycle seat and the passengers sit behind on a two-seater bench.

Where to shop

In Cuba's cities there are large shopping malls, small stores, and markets where people buy fresh food and supplies. Some items are in short supply, such as meat and milk. To ensure that all Cubans get an equal amount of these supplies, the government set up a rationing system. Each month, families receive ration books that allow them to buy a certain number of goods at state-run stores. The government is also working to improve agriculture, industry, and its relationships with other countries to fill these shortages.

(left) Buildings in older parts of Cuba, especially in La Habana Vieja, or Old Havana, are being restored with the help of the Cuban government and international organizations, such as the United Nations Educational, Scientific, and Cultural Organization (UNESCO).

Some Cubans travel in vehicles called camellos, *which means "camels." The vehicles are made from two buses welded together. They get their nickname because they look like two-humped camels.*

Time to learn

All education is free in Cuba, as are textbooks, lunches, and transportation to and from school. Education and teachers are so valued in Cuba that there is a holiday called *El Día del Maestro*, or "Teachers' Day," on December 22. On this day, children have parties where they give their teachers flowers and other gifts. Dancing, playing games, and eating special treats are also part of the fun.

School days

Children go to school from age five to fourteen. They begin their school day with the chant "Be Like Che" to remind them of Che Guevara's ideas of strength and independence. Students also salute the flag and sing Cuba's national anthem.

Between grades one and six, children study subjects such as math, science, music, history, Spanish, physical education, and geography. They also help care for school gardens and orchards, and do daily chores to help keep schools clean.

Basic secondary and high schools

Basic secondary school lasts for three years, from grade seven to nine. After grade nine, children go to high school for three years. Some high schools specialize in certain subjects, such as science, teaching, sports, or the arts.

The government believes that all students in basic secondary and high schools should learn about Cuba's agriculture. Students in the countryside work in the school's fields for part of the day, while students in the city spend five to seven weeks each year in an *escuela en el campo*, or school in the countryside. They spend half the day studying in the classroom and the other half growing crops and caring for animals.

(above) Students clear a field of weeds and stones so it can be plowed and planted for the new harvest. Working in the fields not only teaches students about the country's agriculture, but it also saves money on labor, which helps the government pay for free education.

(left) Children wear uniforms to school. Most uniforms consist of khaki, red, or blue pants or a skirt, a white shirt, and a blue or red neckerchief.

After high school

After high school, some students get jobs, while others continue their education at university, where they study subjects such as science and medicine. Still other students go to teachers' colleges or technical schools, where they learn to build and fix items such as computers.

Television in education

Each Cuban classroom has a television set so that students can watch educational programs broadcast on the country's three national TV channels. Recently, the government started a television station that only broadcasts educational programs. One program, *La universidad para todos*, or "University for Everyone," teaches subjects studied in Cuba's universities to people who are not in school, but are interested in learning.

Bringing learning to the people

Before the revolutionary government took power, many people in Cuba's countryside areas were illiterate, which means they did not know how to read or write. There were either no schools nearby or people could not attend because they had to work in the fields.

Groups of teachers, known as literacy brigades, traveled through the countryside during the early 1960s to teach as many Cubans as possible. Some older students took time off from their studies to help teach in the brigades. The brigades are no longer needed because education is more available. The government has built more schools and now offers adults who wish to further their education classes in English, art, business, and other subjects. Ninety-nine percent of Cubans can now read and write.

Students relax on the steps of the Universidad de La Habana, or Havana University, which was founded in 1728.

Foreign students

Cuba has invited students from other parts of the world, such as Africa, **Latin America**, and the Caribbean, to attend its schools. More than 15,000 students from Africa have studied on a full **scholarship** on Isla de la Juventud, or Isle of Youth, off Cuba's southwestern coast. The island was once home to more than 60 schools, many of which are still open today. Cuba has also established a Latin American School of Medicine, where more than 10,000 students from all over the Americas, including some from the United States, study free of charge.

Students in Santa Lucía, in the northeast, prepare to watch a lecture at their technical college. Educational programs are broadcast over the Internet in Cuba.

Throughout Cuba, people cycle, swim, hike, and play sports, such as baseball, basketball, and *fútbol*, or soccer. Sporting events in Cuba are funded by the government. This means that people can see their favorite athletes or teams for little money.

Marathon runners carrying the Cuban flag prepare to race through the streets of Havana.

Take me out to the ball game

In the 1700s, sailors from the United States taught Cubans to play baseball while their ships were docked in Cuba's harbors. Today, baseball is the most popular sport on the island. Cuban children begin playing in baseball leagues as early as age seven. Many of them hope to join professional city teams or become members of Cuba's national team. Several Cuban baseball players have left Cuba to play with professional teams in the United States. Tony Pérez is one of the best known Cuban baseball players. He won the World Series in 1975 and 1976 with the Cincinnati Reds and was inducted into the U.S. Baseball Hall of Fame in 2000.

Ball sports

Basketball, volleyball, and *fútbol* are popular sports in Cuba. Most people play for fun, but others play professionally. Cuba also has a professional *fútbol de sala*, or court football, team. *Fútbol de sala* is similar to soccer, but it is played indoors or outdoors on courts the same size as those used for basketball. Two five-person teams try to kick a ball that is heavier and less bouncy than a soccer ball into the opposing team's net.

Friends in a Havana neighborhood practice batting in a baseball game.

Sports schools

Each year, coaches in elementary schools select outstanding athletes to attend special sports training schools. Children at these schools study regular subjects in the mornings and practice their sports in the afternoons. After two or three years, the best athletes move up to an Escuela Superior Provincial de Atletismo (ESPA), or Higher Provincial School for Sports Development, where they continue their studies and practice their sports. The best athletes go on to play for Cuba's national teams.

Students play soccer during recess. Some of them hope to join Cuba's national soccer team, which plays in worldwide competitions.

Other sports and games

Many Cubans attend boxing matches. Boys first learn this sport in school, and are encouraged to enter local tournaments if they have a talent for it. Cubans also play *jai alai*, which the Spanish introduced to the island. To play *jai alai*, two to four players play on a three-sided court. Each player uses a 24-inch (60-centimeter) *cesta*, or wicker glove, strapped to his or her hands to throw a small, hard ball against the wall as hard and fast as possible. The goal is to throw the ball in such a way that the other player cannot catch and return it.

Las cuatro esquinas

Cuban children play hide-and-seek in city parks, go inline skating, and fly colorful paper kites on windy days. They also play a game called *las cuatro esquinas*, or "the four corners." Players stand on four street corners, or between four rocks or trees, and one player stands in the center. The players on the corners run from one corner to another, signaling to each other with a gesture or look when they want to exchange places. The goal of the game is for the player in the center to steal one of the empty corners as the other players switch positions. The player who loses his or her corner moves to the center.

Most towns have at least one gymnasium where weekend wrestling matches are held, and temporary rings are set up in plazas for tournaments. Cuba's best wrestlers participate in the wrestling World Championships, which are held in a different country each year.

Dominoes

Dominoes is a popular game played with a set of rectangular pieces, also called dominoes. Each domino is divided into two, with a different number of pips, or dots, in each part. The object of the game is for players to lay dominoes side by side so that the number of pips on the right side of one domino is the same as the number of pips on the left side of the next domino. The first player to get rid of all his or her dominoes wins.

Cuban runner Ana Fidelia Quirot has won several world track competitions, as well as a silver medal in the 1996 Olympic games.

Cubans play a lot of chess. Chess players move different pieces around a board until one player captures the other player's most important piece, the king.

Rodeos

A rodeo takes place in Havana almost every Sunday. *Vaqueros*, or cowboys, participate in competitions to show off their skills. In one event, "bulldoggers," who wear red crash helmets, leap from their horses onto the horns of galloping bulls and try to wrestle them to the ground. In wild-cow milking, pairs of cowboys run from one end of an arena to the other to grab the nearest cow. As one cowboy in each pair steadies the animal, the other tries to get a few squirts of milk into a tin cup without getting kicked. Then, the pair tries to be the first to reach the announcer without spilling any milk.

The tastes of Cuba

Each group of people who settled in Cuba introduced flavors to the island that became part of Cuban cooking. The Spanish brought *bacalao*, which is cod that is dried and salted. *Bacalao a la vizcaína* is battered salt cod served with a sauce of sweet peppers, garlic, onion, and potatoes. Africans introduced vegetables such as okra and fruits such as plantains, which look like large bananas but are not sweet. *Tostones* are plantains that are fried, flattened, and then fried again to make them extra crispy.

Criollo

Traditional Cuban cuisine is called *criollo*, or Creole. Many *criollo* dishes, especially soups and rice dishes, are made with red, white, or black beans. Cuba's national dish, *moros y cristianos*, is a mixture of black beans and rice. Baked, fried, or boiled plantains, yuca, and sweet potatoes are other staples of the Cuban diet. Favorite vegetables include corn and *calabaza*, which is similar to squash.

A woman fries malanga, *a root vegetable served with many Cuban dishes.*

Daily meals

Cubans usually begin the day with crusty bread, butter, cheese, fruit juice, and *café con leche*, which is coffee with heated milk. Lunch consists of *frijoles negros y arroz*, which is a black bean soup with rice, or *arroz con pasas y huevos*, which consists of raisins and rice with a fried egg on top. Dinner usually includes a meat dish, with rice, beans, and vegetables. Delicious desserts include *casquito de guayaba con queso*, or jam made from guava fruit served with a slice of mild cheese, *helado*, or ice cream, *coco quemado*, which is a coconut cake, and *churros*, a twisted stick of fried dough sprinkled with sugar.

Fresh fruits and vegetables, such as bananas, tomatoes, carrots, and cucumbers, grow in Cuba.

A special Cuban meal includes crispy fried chicken, potatoes, and tostones, or plantains.

Ensalada de aguacate y piña

Cubans eat many types of *ensalada de aguacate*, or avocado salad. In this recipe, *piña*, or pineapple, is added. You can make this salad for eight people with an adult's help.

You will need:
2 large avocados
2 cups (500 ml) fresh or canned pineapple in cubes
Juice of one lemon or lime
1/2 cup (125 ml) olive oil
salt and freshly ground pepper

1. Cut the avocado into bite-sized cubes.
2. Mix the avocado and pineapple pieces in a bowl.
3. Sprinkle lemon or lime juice and olive oil over the mixture.
4. Toss lightly and season with salt and pepper.

Meat and seafood

Cubans eat a lot of fish and a small amount of beef, pork, and chicken, which are in short supply. A favorite dish is *ropa vieja*, which means "old clothes." It is made with shredded steak and looks like cloth rags. *Picadillo* is a mix of ground beef and green peppers, onions, tomatoes, and olives. *Fufú* is a mix of mashed green bananas served with crumbled pork rinds. *Lechón asado* is a whole roast suckling pig that is served at large parties and celebrations. Favorite chicken dishes include *pollo fricasé*, which is **fricasseed** chicken, *pollo a la parrilla*, which is grilled chicken, and *pollo asado*, which is roast chicken.

Drinks

Many Cubans enjoy drinks made from fruits that grow on the island, such as mangoes, papayas, coconuts, limes, and lemons. Several beverages are made with sugar cane, including a clear juice called *guarapo* and an alcoholic beverage called rum. Another favorite drink is Cuban coffee. People brew, or make, it very strong and add a lot of sugar for sweetness.

Friends enjoy a drink of rum at a tavern, or bar, in Havana.

Food shortages

Cuba has faced many food shortages since the beginning of the United States' trade embargo and the fall of the U.S.S.R. Today, the Cuban government is trying to find new sources of food. It is reducing the number of sugar cane crops and, instead, is growing other food, such as citrus fruit. It is also producing different foods, such as soy milk, soy yogurt, and a meat substitute called tofu. These foods are from the soybean plant, which grows easily in Cuba's climate. To increase their supply of food, many Cubans grow their own fruits and vegetables on small plots of land in the countryside and in public gardens in cities.

Restaurants sell snacks, such as bocaditos, *which are ham and cheese sandwiches.*

A vendor places yuca, a root vegetable, into a woman's bag at a market.

Manuel loves baseball so much he plays every day.

It was 8:00 on a Saturday morning when Manuel ran into the kitchen, excited to start his day. "*Buenos días*, Manuel," his mother, Soledad, said. Manuel's father smiled as he sipped his *café con leche*.

"*Buenos días, Mamá, Papá*," Manuel replied as he quickly swallowed some bread and cheese. His mother offered to prepare him a fried egg, but he said, "*No, gracias*." He was too excited to eat more. Besides, he wanted to finish his chores so that he, his father, and their neighbors could leave for the baseball game. The home team, Santiago de Cuba, was playing a team from Havana.

Manuel went down to the community garden to water his family's fruits and vegetables. They would be delicious fresh or cooked in soups.

"Can we go now? Is it time to go?" Manuel asked his father eagerly as he ran back into the apartment.

"Yes," his father replied. "It may take us some time to get there. Run next door and see if Jorge is ready."

"*Adiós, Mamá*," Manuel said, kissing his mother's cheek. She was a teacher, and she planned to spend the morning marking her students' essays.

Manuel ran down the hall to get Jorge. Jorge opened the door even before Manuel knocked.

"Ready to go?" Manuel asked. "Of course I am," Jorge replied, and he grabbed his baseball mitt from a table by the door.

Manuel and Jorge had been to several baseball games together. It was their favorite sport. They played baseball on their school team, and on weekends they played with their friends in the schoolyard or park.

The boys and their fathers took the bus to the baseball stadium. When they arrived, they made their way through the crowds of cheering fans to their seats, passing posters with slogans that inspired Cubans to play sports.

As the game began, everyone clapped along to the music of the *conga* bands scattered throughout the stands. The bands also beat out their rhythms while the home team was batting.

Manuel turned to his father and asked, "Do you think I might be a good enough baseball player to go to a sports school one day?"

His father grinned, "That would be great, wouldn't it? You'd get a good education and have a chance to improve at baseball!"

The baseball game was one of the most exciting Manuel had ever seen. It was the top of the ninth inning, and the score was tied at two. Manuel held his breath as Santiago's pitcher struck out one Havana batter, then another, and then a third. It was Santiago's last inning at bat. The team had to score a run, otherwise the game would go into extra innings. Sure enough, Santiago's very first batter hit a home run. Santiago won the game!

The crowd began to chant wildly, "Santiago, Santiago!" as Manuel, Jorge, and their fathers left the stadium. By the time they got home, Manuel's mother had finished marking her students' essays and had prepared a light dinner of *congri*, which is rice with red kidney beans, and a green salad. Manuel gobbled it down and then jumped up from the table.

"Where are you going?" his mother asked. "I'm going to play baseball with Jorge, of course!" Manuel waved, and then headed off to find his friend so they could replay the entire Santiago-Havana game.

Crowds of people wait for the bus to downtown Santiago.

On their way home from the baseball game, Manuel, Jorge, and their fathers pass a patio filled with tourists drinking, eating, and chatting with friends.

Glossary

ally A country that helps another country, especially during a war

ancestor A person from whom one is descended

archaeologist A person who studies the past by looking at buildings and artifacts

cease-fire An agreement between two countries to stop fighting and discuss peace

colonist A person who lives in a settlement controlled by a distant country

Communist Relating to an economic system where a country's natural resources, businesses, and industry are owned by all the people and controlled by the government

conquistador A Spanish conqueror who defeated people in the New World

constitution A set of rules, laws, or customs of a government

descended Having roots to a certain family or group

dictator A ruler with complete power

economy The way a country organizes and manages its business, industries, and money

embargo A government order not to trade with another country

emigration Leaving one country for another

fricasseed Prepared by cutting into chunks and stewing in gravy

gourd The hard-shelled fruit of certain vines

import To buy goods from another country

invader A person who enters using force

invest To give money to companies in exchange for a percentage of the profits

Latin America The Spanish-, French-, and Portuguese-speaking countries south of the U.S.

lease To rent property

merchant A person who buys and sells goods

nationalist Wanting independence for one's country

naval base A center for a large force of warships and military personnel

nuclear missile A weapon, fired at a target, that gets its force from the splitting of atoms

plantation A large farm on which crops such as cotton and sugar are grown

profit Money kept after all business costs are paid

rebellion An uprising against a government or ruler

revolutionary A person who helps overthrow a government

Roman Catholicism A denomination of Christianity, led by the Pope in Rome

saint A person through whom God performs miracles according to the Christian Church

scholarship Money given to students to help them pay for their studies

smuggle To bring something in or out of a country illegally

standard of living The level of comfort and wealth of a society

visa A document that allows a person to visit or work in another country

 # Index